What did you eat for Dinner?

Written by Miguel Hartford

Illustrated by JRaphael Honasan

Lovett Press International
214-350-1696

ISBN: 978-1-937045-22-7

To see other books by this author, visit:
Hartfordbooks.com

Contact the author directly at:
Migueldenisia@hotmail.com

Illustrator: JRaphael Edmundo Honasan
jraphaelhonasan@gmail.com

Dedication

*To my family at Mr. Baker's Man.
I'm glad to see your dreams come true.*

Mr. Gipson told the class, "I ate Mofongo for dinner last night." Then he asked, "Does anyone know what that is?"

"I do," Juan says. "It's Puerto Rican food with plantains and spices."

"Do you eat it with shrimp or chicken?" Mr. Gipson asks.
"My mom likes shrimp best, but I'll take chicken for the win," Juan says. Mr. Gipson says, "Let's go around the room and everyone can tell me what they ate for dinner last night."

"It's springtime, so my dad is back on the grill. The hamburgers were the best topped with pickles that were sour or dill. His chicken, hot dogs and saucy ribs, are the best around and no one fibs," Michelle says.

Kody said, "Last night, my mom cooked spaghetti and baked ziti. She made it from scratch, using old family recipes."
Aidan went next, "We ate salad and homemade pizza with veggies."

"We had macaroni, peas and chicken golden fried," Derrick said.
Niya said, "We had steak and potatoes with grilled shrimp and lobster on the side."

"Wow. I wish I had been at your place. After eating all that, I would've had the widest smile on my face," Mr. Gipson said.

"We don't eat like that every night. My mom had colleagues over, so she really served us right," Niya said.

Zoey said, "Last night we had fish and chips."
"You had potato chips for dinner? You mean like salsa chips and dip?" Juan asked.
"No," Zoey laughs. "In England, chips mean French fries," she explains.
"Well for me, chips mean tortilla chips. My aunt, uncle and cousins came over. We had a feast of chips and salsa, queso dip, tacos, quesadillas, burritos and rice," Juan says.

Kaitlyn says, "We went to a buffet. I ate plate after plate of crab legs on ice." "Monday and last night we had meatloaf, which I'm tired of since we've had it twice," Alyssa says.

"We had meat and lo mein noodles," Misa says.
Dietrich says, "We caught and cooked salmon.
My mom says it's good for the brain."
"Last night we ate jerk chicken," Delonn says.

"Last night we had Riz et Pios Rouges," Emma says.
"What's that?" Misa asks.
"It's rice and red beans," Emma says and laughs.
Johari explains, "I had Jollof rice and Iyan with isu,
which are yams. Plus, homemade biscuits that I love
with blackberry jam."

"We ate a soup from beef called Khash," Hana says.
Jaylen says, "Dinner was delicious at my house. All of my family loves succotash."
"Mine too," Michelle says.
"What's that?" Reina asks.
"It's a red sauce with okra, corn, tomatoes, sausage and shrimp. My dad tells my mom add extra meat because she tends to scrimp," Jaylen says.

Arjul says, "My mom and grandmother make the best chicken curry."

"Last night I made dinner. I fixed sushi by myself. Dad told me not to hurry," Akira says.

"We had Bossam and steamed vegetables with pork. It was sister's pick. She says it's one of the best dishes to touch chopsticks," Daniel says.

Kylie said, "We had my aunt's vegetable soup. I ate meat, fruit, vegetables, and bread and drank milk. That's every food group."

"My mom made shrimp salad with lettuce, radishes, cucumbers and tomatoes," Zoey says.

Bryce says, "My mom loves seafood. We had boiled crawfish and potatoes."
"We ate at my grandmother's house last night. She made Kuala pork. It smelled so good in the pot. I was mad that I had to wait because it was so hot," Reina says.

"We all eat different things and they're all great. Last night you had dinner. Tell us what you ate."

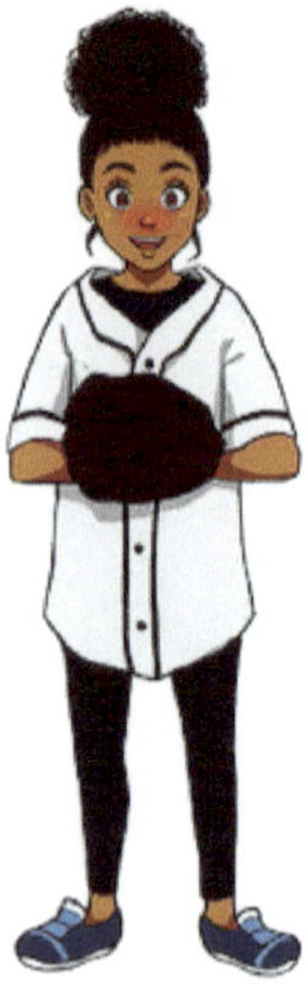

Michelle

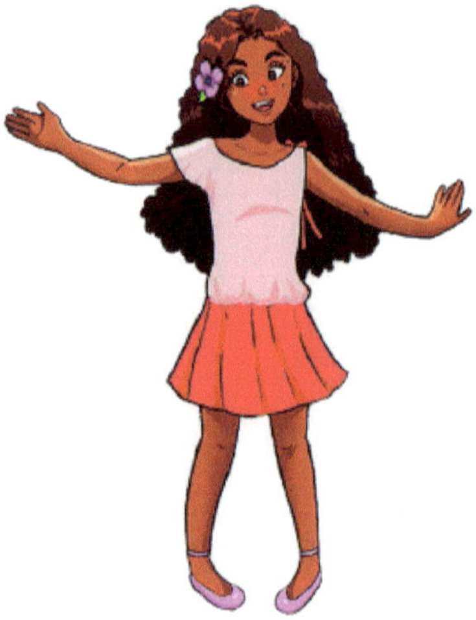

Reina

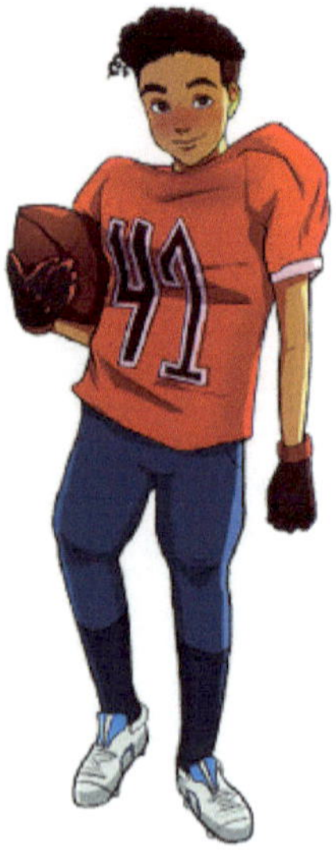

Bryce

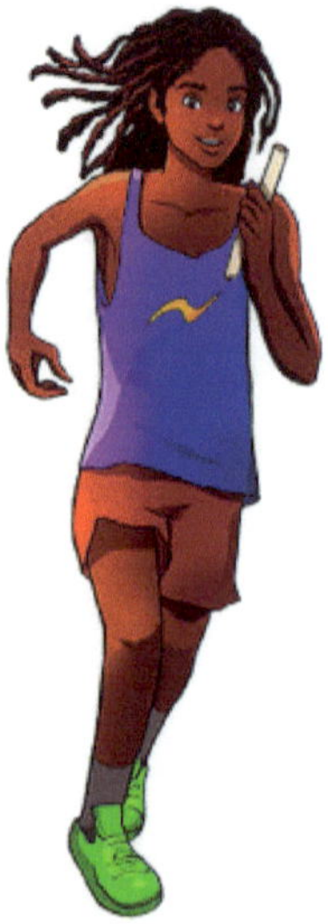

Delonn

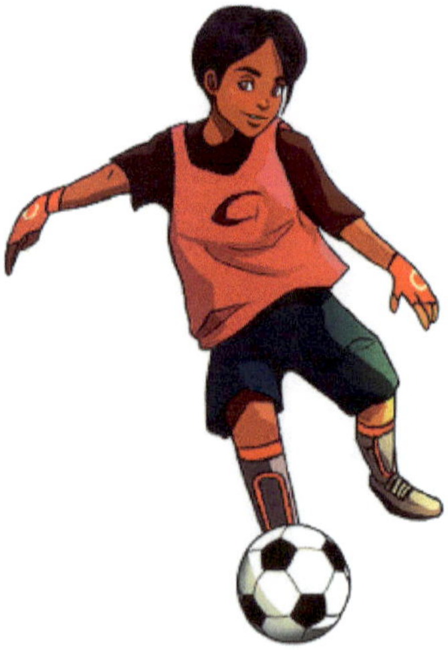

Juan

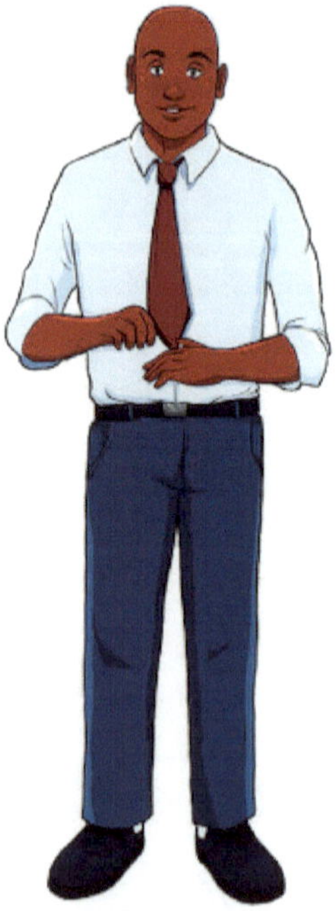

Gipson

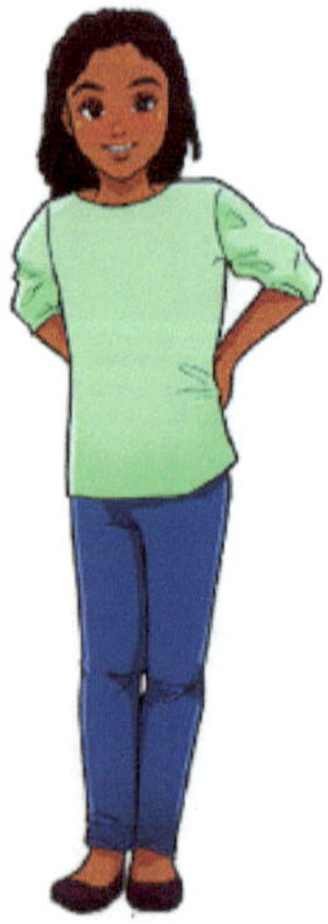

Misa

Aidan

Johari

Alyssa

Niya

Arjun

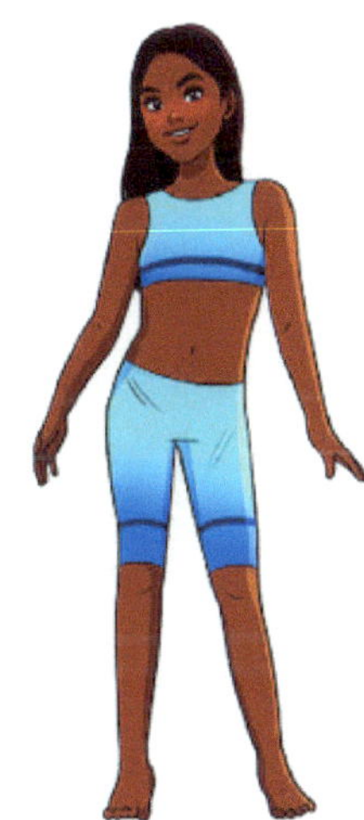

Hana

Jaylen

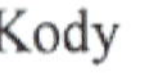

Kody

Dietrich

Emma

Kaitlyn

Daniel

Zoey

Kylie

Culture Kids Series

The Culture Kids series focuses on some attributes and customs of children due to their specific cultures and explores their differences and likenesses.

Books in the Series

Where Do You Go After School?

What Did You Eat for Dinner?

The Best of My Culture

Careers—The Future Me

Traveling and Vacations

What is Art?

Money Management

Other Book Series by Miguel Hartford

Time with Tristan Series

The Time with Tristan series is about a preschool age boy. The series focuses on Tristan and his relationships with family and friends, and encourages children in healthy relationships.

Ingenious Caleb Series

The Ingenious Caleb series focuses on a preschool age boy Caleb and his learning, adventures and relationships with family and friends.

Proof